WIFE

ALSO BY TIPHANIE YANIQUE

How to Escape from a Leper Colony: A Novella and Stories (2010)
I am the Virgin Islands – with Moses Djeli (poetry and photographs for
     children)
Land of Love and Drowning: A Novel (2014)

TIPHANIE YANIQUE

WIFE

PEEPAL TREE

First published in Great Britain in 2015
Peepal Tree Press Ltd
17 King's Avenue
Leeds LS6 1QS
UK

ISBN 13: 9781845232948

Supported using public funding by
ARTS COUNCIL
ENGLAND

She casts her best, she flings herself.

— Coventry Patmore, from *The Angel in the House*

CONTENTS

I.   Notes for Couples Therapy

Dangerous Things   11
Blood Wedding   12
Body Logic   13
Bastard on the Elevated Train   14
Zuihitsu for the Day I Cheat on My Husband, to my fiancé   15
lookout music   18
Dictionary   19
I try   20
A note to the couple's therapist   23
Therapy for a Messiah Complex   24
To Fall or Fly   26
Things the Baby Put into His Mouth   27

.

II.   Altar Calls

A poem to mark when we were afraid   31
African Animal   32
The Husband Speaks from the Mountain   34
Gods and Monsters   35
We Fall out of the Sky   36
A Prelude to Divorce in a Happy Marriage   37
Eight Weeks as Frida   38
A Slave in the House   39
Altar Call   40

III.   Abandonment Stations

My brother comes to me   45
The Falling Out   46
Chief Priestess Say   47

Everybody needs a white husband   49
Last Yanique Nation   50
Feminist Methodology: a found poem   51
Divorce Myth   52
The Baby Abandonment Station   53

IV.   Words (last, fighting, true, etc.)

Cock   57
The Story of Our Elopement   58
Confession of the Five Foolish Brides   61
Chiron and Astraea   62
Suegra   63
God is Not Broken   64
Traditional Virgin Islands Wedding Verse   65
To Capture Ghosts   67

I

NOTES FOR COUPLES THERAPY

Dangerous Things

This is the island.
It is small and vulnerable,
it is a woman, calling. You love her
until you are a part of her
and then, just like that,
you make her less than she was
before – the space
that you take up
is a space where she cannot exist.
It is
something in her history
that does this,
don't mind
her name. The island
is a woman, therefore
dangerous things live below,
beautiful things, also – which can be the most dangerous.
True, we will never be
beyond our histories.
And so I am the island.
And so this is a warning.

Blood Wedding

There is always blood at a wedding
its mirror bright like the rise of a pulse
and the flesh that goes with it   What is
a marriage but a mirror   Yes there is blood
at every wedding   A kind of reaching
for the knife via one's own chest
The heart is removed and it leaves
behind the cavity of necessity

There is more than blood after the wedding
There are bones   There are words
There is a love not found in the heart
but the kidney   A spouse is only a surgeon
passing her own organ through the mirror

      dear
      beautiful
      kidney

A marriage is a myth cleaved
from the mirror   And that is life
despite the phantoms of all us amputees

Body Logic

(after Smith and Hayes)

The body has its own
infant logic.
Its own way to know
if what you speak is true.
It knows where your hands have been.
The body has jokes on you.
The body lies, for real.
It will rat you out.
Give you a negative
when you least
expect it.
The body will fail you, it will betray you.
The body tells you this is love – but hold on,
that's no lie after all.
Picture this, baby: the body's on your side.
It will open you
and leave you open.
And you'll have to read it
like a sonogram.

Bastard on the elevated train

I see Chicago at the second floor,
me, the eldest, on electric gridding,
my noise like a trashcan and not like a train
while the full families settle in.
Not neon lights or taxi cabs, but living rooms,
bright red walls and compact kitchens,
TVs flashing blue onto children's faces.
Round canvases of primary colours. Play pens.
Squat worktables held together with iron bolts.
Shaggy orange carpets. Green tiled floors.
Large bevelled mirrors. A man, never my father,
looks through his window at me.
If there was no glass, I could touch Chicago.
But I am on the outside, being secreted by.

Zuihitsu for the day I cheat on my husband, to my fiancé

I will write
in my journal:

"My lover is warm to my body. Like hair, he covers me.

I could remember my husband meeting me on the mountain.
Hitching with another man's wife. This is before he is my husband.
On the phone, I tell him: when you arrive, please grab me and hold
me. And then when he and the wife arrive I see her first. She is
beautiful and my heat is eager. When I see my husband, who is not
yet my husband, he opens his arms like oars. Cleaves me onto him
and lowers me. Everyone is watching!

I will say my husband is like skin. The imperfect container of things.
Yes, shedding, but always growing back.

Skin: When it splits, there is bleeding. When it breaks, the vitals tumble out.

Will I call him Baby?

I could remember the time my cousin, in her effort to inherit the
house, locked our old aunt out so she would die. I could recall how
my husband, who is not yet my husband, held my head in his lap as
I howled against the fireworks – their beauty bursting – though
nothing but light and gunshots, into the horror of what family can be.

The lover will be the kind that blows his horn and makes my body
shake and sing. "Oh Baby!" I will call out when I'm coming.

Perhaps wives who have sex with men not their husbands are afraid
of growing old. Not to themselves, but to someone else. This is what
I believe. It is nice to be a princess to someone again after being the
queen.

Queen: The title a husband gives to his wife only after first giving it to his own mother.

I could remember, at a time I was deciding which man to marry, that I watched the film *Bridges of Madison County* with one of my possible husbands. I wept. Thinking, already, of the day this one would become the lover. Mourning already, the pummelled beauty of our affair. This one, who would not become my husband, asked why I cried so, and I could not tell him that I would not marry him but that I would take him as a lover when a lonely day came.

My husband, who is not yet my husband, says family is just people. Why expect anything else from them but what you can expect from people? And I say, but I want you to be my family. This is how I propose.

Husband: Next of kin.

Will the lover ever call me Baby?

The best love stories are the ones of infidelity. Faithfulness is a narrative so small. This is why, my husband will say, polyamority seems unpoetic. Jealousy loses its only use. The metaphor is more like having children, whom in vain you vow to love equally. Loving a spouse, says my husband who is not yet my husband, is like praising One God, whom you will betray. In the end, all the others are glittering lumps of fake gold. This is called sin.

Adultery: A fetish for monogamists.

I will tell Baby that I do not want people. I want family. Your husband, he will say, is your family, right? And I cannot tell if he is directing me to remain unattached or if he is pleading with me to adopt him.

My husband, who is not yet my husband, brought flowers. On the stairs, we kissed like the lost. Then he watched me walk into the subway and said, I can't wait to fuck you. It was our first date.

Perhaps, men who have sex with other men's wives are skimpy on soul. Their spines too fragile to carry folk on their own. They love prodigally. Still, I will fall for the lover and fuck him because that is what we wives do."

When I am found out I will say to my husband:

Marriage is a form of worship.

look out music

it seems to me
that people should
say what they
want
the thing that
matters
because what
is there to lose?
except your own
soul
and what's that
up against any
man's history?

Dictionary

wife – (European origins) a married woman. As in slave in the house. As in chef, maid, nanny and prostitute. But unpaid for these services. A woman defined in relation to her spouse, generally a man. In the colloquial, wife means woman: as in "Old wives' tale" meaning a story passed down by ignorant old women. As in "She's my wife, not my mistress and so did not receive a fur for Christmas. Instead, I bought her a vacuum cleaner, which she loved."

wifey – (American Negro origins) diminutive of wife but more desirable. Girl who cooks, cleans, fucks and gives back massages. As in, "I took this girl home to my moms and she brought potato salad instead of a bottle of wine – because she's a good wifey and knows better." Woman to have sex with but to whom you are not married, and probably never will marry. Or might marry if she gets pregnant – and then she will become WIFE. If she is not wed at the time of giving birth she will become a "baby mama". A diminutive less desirable for all parties.

get wife – (Caribbean origins) to have sex, to fuck a human female, to be on a mission to have sex. As in "You get wife last night? That must be why you in such a good mood." Or "My woman vex with me and ain give me wife in a week." A man might say to a whore: "I'll give you twenty dollars for the wife." Meaning, I will pay you an inadequate sum to fuck you. "Get" translates loosely to "have". "Wife" is a direct translation of "sex".

to wife – (origins unknown) a feminine specific verb suggesting a woman has convinced a man that she is worthy of romantic and sexual commitment. As in "He promised to wife me but I'm still waiting on the ring." Once the woman has the ring, being wifed may be elevated to "being ringed", as in lassoed, as in good enough that a man would swing a rope around you. Preferably the rope is made of gold and has a diamond at the knot.

I try

(for Jericho)

1.

In the high branches of a tree
there is a bride's
veil
swinging
Of course, there is a story
here

Though, perhaps the veil is nothing
more than a white
garbage bag
But I know better
I don't believe my eyes

2.

We are beneath
the plastic bag in the tree
when he says
"Beware, there is a ghost
in that tree"

Then I know
that I am not alone
with this odd telepathy

3.

Now we may try the ghost bride
for answers

Such as
what do dead bodies mean
when swaying
from trees?

A note to the couple's therapist

My self-diagnosis: It's just this body
I was given.
It wants to be more.
Now it smells like rust
but I'm too young
to flake away.
Now, when I'm touched
it's with a thrusting motion
as though my body
were no more than
a pail of water,
a warm place
to wash one's hands.
But if I'm rust, I want to come off
on fingers, leave a stain.
And if I am water then I plan to be the ocean.
I'll leave salt behind.

Therapy for a Messiah Complex

1.

The water is a wall. We walk through
the sea on dry ground.
But we will not lose our way through the desert.

2.

Moses knows that we worship
the calf. Still,
he brings the lice and the locusts.
He brings the frogs and the death of the firstborn.
Moses quarrels with the burning bush inside himself.
But we will not be impressed with staffs turned into cobras.

3.

Baby Jesus
needs us.
His halo is heavy.
The glow pushes
through the pores
on His little head.
It hurts. Easy hands soil His hem. And His infant feet.
But when He is dirty we will bathe Baby Jesus in the river.

4.

When Moses brings down the commandments
Baby Jesus crayons over them in earthy colours.
When we spank Baby Jesus,
He weeps. He weeps.
But we will not be impressed with water turned into wine.

5.

The Lord says:
My child has the self-centredness of an only son.
My servants make such sinful mistakes,
be it at the hand of Pharaoh or Pharisees.

But we will not hire Judas to hold the money.
We will know better. We will release the sea.

To Fall or Fly

I want to survive my Diego. My own ugly older man who degrades
me but loves me like a photograph. Loves me only when I obey, like
the click, like smile and say cheese. He loves his own pregnant belly.
Hides in it while I do the pushing. Still, I wanted him worse than a
broken spinal cord. So it only followed that I would call him Daddy
and allow him to outlive me, despite his age. Tell me how to survive.
Must our kind choose love over love? Me? I hope to return. I wish
to get it right. I don't mind the pain. I did it smart. I wouldn't wear
the peasant dress. But I sucked him into tears. I taped myself below
the pictures. He told me I wasn't art, but I refused to give in to his
fear. I wanted to be printed into postcards so he could carry me to
Zimbabwe or Zaire. I am the one, the one. Oh. The truth is I don't
want to survive. I want to die of my Diego. I want to be remembered
for it. But I've forgotten his fear of flying. And flying suggests falling.
And falling suggests love. I so desire that picture. I should have been
better warned. A sign in the corner of a painting, that loneliness is a
selfish sin. But dying of heartbreak is a betrayal of all the comman-
dants at once. Hold on. That's Diego coming around the corner. No,
no it's only my reflection. Put a frame around the mirror. It's me.
It's all and only me.

Things the baby put into his mouth

Your shoe, my shoe and the baby's own shoes, all with the grime of street baked into the bottom

The small bright pencil sharpener, with a little fleck of lead peeking out from the blade of its box

The fat tape we used to flatten down the nails, now spooled out to its cardboard core and its jagged razor

The tiny white book with its twelve brown matches, each waiting to ignite a hungry blazing tip

A stick of long and thick incense with the fragile splint at one end and the ash soft and burning at the other

The chewy black electric cord and glinting steel prong all attached to the heavy glass dome of the blender

II

ALTAR CALLS

A poem to mark when we were afraid

We take the highway.
We arrive at the market for fleas after dark.
We are received as the representatives
from the Pygmy Goat Association.
We are given the portable cabin for lodging.
We stay at the RV Park and Motel.
At the revival the following morning,
a sir makes the announcement concerning
the crossing of cattle and Hummers.
A ma'am passes out bumper stickers that read "Follow me to Christ."
From the official pamphlet we learn:
pygmies are black pagans and the goat is a metaphor.
That night, though you sleep beside me, the steers stamp me into meat.
But we are still safe – it is only all a premonition.

African Animal

The tradition is that as the son grows older
he is driven out.
He keeps to the corners of the community.
But the women refuse him
their shelter or care.
He does not understand what Mama
understands.
That he will turn bull.
Will attack the babies and justify it.
He is just a child himself now.
He trails the women. Longing
for them. Until one morning
they are simply not there.
And he searches. Perhaps
they are hiding. Perhaps they are dead.
But no, they are only just gone
from him. This dismissal is the solution
or it is the sickness.

He eats alone.
He builds himself a home.
He waits for the women
to come. With great hope, he waits.
When one arrives he welcomes her
with dance. A meal.
But she wants a new home. One for lovemaking.
He builds it for her. He uses his imagination.
He spends his worth. He honours her. But she
finds the place unsatisfactory. He builds
another. And another. Until
she relents. Accepts.
When she is with child he becomes nostalgic
for his own childhood.
He remembers his mother and his sisters.

Of course his bride does not stay.
He yearns for a boy child, who will want him.
But he never knows.

When his lover returns, he is too grateful to ask.
Too grateful to note that she has the mark
of many births
on her body. The marks of other bulls.

He will never become accustomed to her leaving.
He will challenge other cast-out sons, in hopes that she
hears of his valour. Loves him.
In battle there is a recognition among the bulls.
Is this his son, now grown and come to challenge him?
Is this his brother?

The Husband Speaks from the Mountain

Not from the mountain, in reality.
Metaphysically, I speak from the bush. Or the desert.
Or something on that level.

I speak of ying and yang. Husband and wife.
Except that, epistemologically, wife only means woman.
See, it's not about a partnership. There's the mistake
in our human thinking:
that we have separate thinking.
Meta-really,
we are one body, mind and all.
But see. Right there? When I do that? That's what I mean.
I felt that. I feel you.

Queen, listen. I know I'm no walk in the park.
Never have been.
But marriage isn't about
courting or canting.
I'm carrying you.
You're pushing me. I'm
not never
going to let you fall.
Feel that? Feel me?

Even the first of my kind
had his Erin. You
see what I'm saying here?
Marriage is desert. Marriage is fire.
You are my burning bush.

See, husband means the one who takes care.
It's not that thorny. Except that it's the most of everything
in the world.
See?
                    Woman, we are the mountain.

Gods and Monsters

(For R. R. McGarrah)

"All trees are pilgrims. They have their Messiah, whom they seek."
—Vladimir Nabokov

Love, I remember we were trees.
We bent and worshipped each other.
God hadn't forgotten us,
after all.
But it's true, I married what saved

me. Then I learned
I am so simple.
I suffer for it.
My simplicity is that of gladiators.
I fight until the lion comes out.
You see, even love has its jaws.
The L. The E.

Soon everything will break
free. Even the trees.

We fall out of the sky

But if we board the plane
I will always fight for us to sit side by side.
If the cabin pressure goes
and the plane plummets like a suicide,
we will learn together what the seat belts are for.
One by one the other passengers will give in
to oxygen, then its absence. But not me,
please know, not me.
I will tie your belt around our waists.
In the coma you cannot help.
I will open your mouth to give you my breath
as the windows burst in.
Perhaps we will never know if
we are dead or lost.

A prelude to divorce in a happy marriage

Nobody believes it, but we
are useless to each
other, first like wet
matches, when we still
had hope that something
would catch, would
light and hold.

Then we were
like used tea bags.
We grew lazy with
water but did not
burst. We were
harmless in this way.
We had done the work
and then seeped a stain
on the dining table.

But now even we
cannot believe our failure
is a wave coming
steadily at them
from behind. They want us
to tell them how
to make forever
but we give direction
from under water.

Eight Weeks as Frida

Sit. I say, stand.
I say body, obey.
I am the steward.
Body, my slave,
my primary lover,
you must manage.
Hold together with straps
and nails, if we must.
Walk. Walk.
I have not been
prudent with my dutiful
body. Body as wife.
Please, sit.
I see feet in the noose,
blood in the head.
I say, stand. I say,
resurrect.

A Slave in the House

I am not someone
to steal with, not someone
to steal away with,
to risk skin to sneak
into the cane,
and make love within the sugar.

I am married to a man without slaves
as ancestors.
He is alone in this new
world. He needs no rescue.

.

Altar Call

> "If you bring forth what is within you,
> what is within you will save you."
> — from *The Gnostic Gospel of St. Thomas*

The first time the man left her he walked down the aisle,
his face blank with hopelessness or with hope.

The preacher had begged for those who wanted Jesus,
and so he was headed towards the altar.

The wife whispered, "Wait, my love,"
but that was not enough up against God calling him come.

That night the man asked her to pray with him.
He recited, as he always did, the Our Father.

She performed the Hail Mary for him
and he lay in her lap like a child.

She claimed him as her bright little boy.
For after the altar, he could not be her man.

For years he believed he would grant her
a mansion, even though he never

managed half their tiny rent.
She learned that truth

was not what he could stand
and so he was never told that the landlord

was her lover. He was never told
that their son, slow, took after him.

The story of their life together
is the same as anyone's.

III

ABANDONMENT STATIONS

My brother comes to me

They are at the red gate
of my grandmother's white house
The gate is taller than them both
The mother, who is my mother, is holding her son's hand
The boy, who is my brother, is only four years old
She, our mother, is going crazy
She wants to take him with her
A blood stain has spread permanently on my brother's white shirt
I am at the steps of the house, like a bride
I am fifteen and calling to my brother, "Come to *me*"
Her teeth are bared They are not pearls
"*I* am your mother," she shouts
We are all crying and all our tears are all different
Our mother's hair is a flame above us

The Falling Out

Mothering is an instinct.
Even dogs
do it. Marriage is contrived
in comparison.
But when one
fails the other turns
away from the claim:
we are human. Then
the married
must chose
myth or
massacre.

Chief Priestess Say

Amen, Amen.

I know where I hope
for a tongue.
Where I hope for something harder.
When my father brings the belt, then
the broom, then the brick
to my back
I know where to run. My lover
saves me from the coffin. Amen, Amen.

Some fathers are angry when their
daughters sleep with men. Per-
haps they want their daughters,
first and then always.

For Fela I bind
each of my legs
with yellow
twine. I knot fresh leaves
into my hair. Amen, Amen.

Wives are fools, but only other
men would figure that.

Now my husband gives me
my turn.
I make my hips
a finger, a curl
to come. When he dances he is all
there is. And I love
him then. Amen, Amen.

Husbands are better lovers than
fathers could ever claim to be.

Our husband says we
are all water. We have no
enemies. Not blood
even. Amen, Amen.

Most men are zombies. In spirit,
it is always the women who carry
the coffin.

Everybody needs a white husband

We all need a little bleach to shine. You can't walk up any
coloured carpet brown on brown. You know you'll disappear.
Can't get a job? Well, you better shackle down
a white husband. Hungry? Thirsty? He can fix that, too. He
can remake God in your image if you ask with the correct
inflections. And best of all, he can give you milky babies with
hair you don't have to be ashamed of.

Believe me, I understand. A husband is meant to be a trophy.
But he can also be a white peace flag. A thing to surrender in
the wind and signal that you can get along. But the trick is
letting him go.

When is the right time to break the news? When is the perfect
moment to admit that marriage is just about your momentum in
the world? Girl, I can't help you there.

Just make sure your kinky pubic hairs leave imprints on his face.
Everyone knows that's a symbol better than a wedding ring.

Last Yanique Nation

The pit in my womb where the doctor lover
says is my self, is not a nation.
My soul is called Che, as in Guevara,
but my body has not died for the nation.
I told my enemy I loved her, as
I love my nation. Guevara,
was no coward, which means he tended towards
fool. I want to be a fool in love and thus
a fool for this nation. My soul doesn't
care about nations. My soul makes its country
in the backyard or bedroom of wherever
I carry it. My islands do not make
a nation. Yet my soul guards
their bodies, their waters. That then
is the nation. Yes, the pink pit
does bear the possibility of nations.
Che rests its teeth into my belly. I feel
the love and remember Guevara;
the man, had no nation but nations.
He died for the end of our nations.
I speak my soul's only language, dear
doctor revolutionary, in the name
of no nation. Despite the proxy
of vows I am both body and nation.

Feminist Methodology: a found poem

Any essay question about sex is controversial.

1. Are you threatened by intimacy or by individuation?
   It is just too difficult to say different without saying better or
   worse. Even I know that if you make a woman out of a man you
   are bound to get nothing more than dust.

2. Be frank, are you a woman or a man?
   Listen, I already fucked the frog and all the seven little men.
   I do not want to marry the prince.
   Leave me with my beautiful mirror and my many dancing
   shoes.

3. Why on earth don't you declare yourself?
   Well, I'm a bitch.
   And there are things in this world not dreamt of in the history.

Divorce Myth

At first the water rose up like a wall.
The kingdom didn't burn down.
The kingdom drowned.
Now in the modern era the wall falls like water.
The sweet water burns away in the flames.

The Baby Abandonment Station

When it was
in Harlem off
the 1 train it was
too easy to get to
if you were a regular
and knew of the twin express.
Even the abandoners expected
a little tribulation so they could
feel the terrible karma of the journey.
So now everyone must take their babies into Brooklyn.   Again
babies get left on platform benches as though waiting for the down
town. No one remembering to whom the baby
belongs. A mother watching from amongst
the other humans. Her fingers gripped
to bone around the rail but her head
turned slightly away like a god.
More often the baby will stay
on the train until
it empties.

IV

WORDS (LAST, FIGHTING, TRUE, ETC.)

Cock

This is you.
The pistol
launched
to the tail
I drink
down
in the roach
darkness.
This is you.
You swell
like a rooster
and I dance
to your
direction.
This is you, love.
Cockier than
first love, love.
Like a cock-
a-too, you said
I could
write this,
but there's
no way
to sing,
not like we do.

The Story of our Elopement

It was the anniversary of the day we met.
And there was also a concert in the park.
Our plan was to marry and then dance
in the grass.

But the carriage
did not take us directly.
First the driver revealed the list:
Communication. Clemency. Conviction.
then released us at the marriage
bureau of Brooklyn.
We refused the undead
roses, the bewitched
box cameras.
We dashed up the stairs,
the white
dress
trembling around me.

We'd forgotten the witness,
and I sensed that the judge,
like a petulant king,
would banish us.
This knowledge grew and then dwarfed
in my chest like an apple
and I wondered if we would make the concert.
We waited inside of walls, gold
as temptation.
We waited and waited
among couples coming together for reasons
not always concerning love.

Afterwards,
we embraced in the chapel

like captives,
until my dress
winged
behind and I was a bird
escaping
us back down the steps
into the freedom
we created. The taxi to Central Park was yellow as straw
or straw turned to gold.
We sat like royalty
in the back seat.
Mine, we said,
and touched the other's
jaw. Mine, to the eyebrow. Mine, to mouth.
That was marriage magic.

But believe it, we missed the concert.
Instead, you promised
me a boat ride after dark.
We laid a blanket upon the earth –
which is a myth
in itself – and ate a picnic in the forest
of trees and skies.
That was our first married meal:
champagne, chevre cheese, clemency.
There was a cello playing its enchantment.
It was not the concert but still
I knelt before the music,
my hand covering my heart.
From your hand you fed the animals.
Our sorcery
was the same.
And we tried not to think of the others at the bureau,
How they almost grew like a riddle
between us.

You planted sticks of incense in a circle.
And either I was the gift
or I was the goddess
as you climbed onto that altar
with me. And the gold sun was dwarfed into stars
winking though the trees.

After dark we wandered to the boats.
But, imagine,
the gate was closed. We shook it like bushes
waiting for fruit
to fall. Conviction.
And the magic was that the gate opened.
We bought the last of the boats and the moon
appeared in the water just as we had wished.
You rowed us to the centre and then beyond
the edge. We were fleeing
to make our own kingdom.
Now any myth
could be true if we communicated it:
I said, I am a princess
I said, you are charming
I said, I will witness
you.

The night we arrived home after eloping
we danced until we were our own end of time.

Confession of the five foolish brides

Ten of us
to start. Tired
with love of you,
half of us fell
to sleep, dreamt deeply.
How could we consider
oil or lamps?
We knew we could feel
our paths
to you. We'd saved ourselves
after all, despite
your delay.
Now we may never be known.
Our bare, tardy palms rap
on the church door.
Our voices call
open, open, Lord.
But did you ever
love us?
We were ready
with our love
if not our light.

Chiron and Astraea

The word is bone.

After the Centaurmachy you were the last left.
I have been dead.
I bear blossoms.
The baby was born in October.
It knew nothing of its own birth
and imagined itself a god – like all babies.
I know so little of my body.
I amazon my own blood.
I bribe my mouth for splinters.

The word is blood.

After the Golden Age I was the last left.
I lost all pain.
I was alone in my sense of October.
The baby was baptized.
It was bathed with dust from the urn.
It was alive and dead – like all babies
I own this scorn.
It becomes me.
I break the river into ashes.

The word is break.

After the wings, hooves, tails, fins and tongues of flame
I grow the head of an eagle, the body of a stallion.
The Cathedral flows among the graffiti.
Every year October is lost again.
I forget that you don't breathe water.
I drag you under.
You bear it.
We eat only bones.
The baby bears the scars of its own blossoming.

Suegra

You can cook in my kitchen.
But you are not allowed to move
the skillet to suit
your right hand instead
of my left.
You have permission to
teach me
how to make his favourite meal.
You may show me his flaws
and trust that I will love him
just the same.
We can conspire.
If your son does dote,
you must
steer him my way.

In the event of a
divorce, he will sneer
that he doesn't know
when I became so
scheming. I shall clarify
in court that I stole the skills
from his mother.
By decree, you won't be
anything to me.
But in Spanish
the title does not involve
the law. You would retain
your own sweet name.

God is not broken

Husband, you have bruises
on your lips from calmly swallowing fire.
Your lab coat
is flammable from too much wear.
When I whisk it away for cleaning
you study the window of the washing machine.
You note that the blood stains at
the stitching reads like an epilogue.

In the surgery
my healing is at the brackish points.
The needle sinks into my foot like a lover
and sits until I scream.

Wild subjects despise the doctor.
Yet, in recovery,
I want to fly inside your patient body.
You offer me the moat of your mouth.

Traditional Virgin Islands Wedding Verse

(for Hannah and James)

When you are born
you are passed to your father's arms
or your mother's chest.
Your parents claim you. You belong
to them. Before you even know
you are your own,
you know that you are
someone else's. You are
bonded. You need to belong.

Then you belong
to the land, the town
in which you are raised. You belong
to the city you choose.
These places have a hold
on you. They claim you.
I am from, you say.
I am of.

Perhaps you belong
to the school. To the church.
You say I am, and name
what you do for sustenance.
These things own you and
you own them.

You are part of a tribe.
It is not a shackle. It is the true story
of self-creation.
It is what makes you.
You come to belong to yourself.

You say I am
and call your own name.

And now
you belong
to each other.
You are of the same tribe.
I am his wife,
you will say; and
I am her husband.
You are future ancestors of
the same village.

And you have made this so
by your own choice.

You will weld yourself
with regard to each other
and because of each other.
You will weave your own self
to the other. You are now native
to each other. You say
I am
yours.
I claim you.

To Capture Ghosts

(for Jean-Michel Basquiat and Moses Djeli)

Dear Samo,

I travelled all the way from the Virgin Islands to find the love of my life. But I got lost in the graveyard. A tour guide said, "I'll take you to him. But you mustn't think I'm a pervert." So I leapt into that man's car and he drove me through the city of your cemetery. And in it I had to find you. Even though I can't even find my mother when I go home. And me and this man, we drove and we drove. And we picked up a middle-aged woman. And we picked up a dog with a collar. And we picked up a stray cat. The dog and the cat seemed indifferent to each other. And still we drove. The man kept saying, "Wait, wait, there is something I must show you" and we would veer repeatedly down a little dead path and he'd tell us the story of a civil war drummer boy shot down by friendly fire, or he'd tell us the story of the hotdog king and he'd point to the hotdog king's palace of a tomb. And all I could wonder was why the hotdog king got a palace but we couldn't get to the other side of the hill, to you. I wanted to cry because here I was on a hill in a cemetery, overlooking a Manhattan that resembled a child with two teeth missing, with a pervert and a woman who didn't say much, except, "Thank you, thank you for taking me on this trip," and of course, the dog and the cat. And we kept veering off to graves of fascination to the man. At one tomb there was a huge Saint Theresa in rapture, and the man got out and beckoned us come. The woman followed him, but I stayed in the car and changed into mourning clothes while the cat and the dog peeped. When the man and the woman returned they stared at me in my black dress and black stockings and black high heels. "You've changed so quickly," he said. "You're like a super hero," she said. And it dawned on me that I am incredible. And that this driving man might desire me like any pervert should and this grateful woman might be my mother and perhaps the dog and the cat would come along as substitutes for children. I wondered if it would rain. And if it did I would know that everything was just right. I so love pathetic

67

fallacy. But it didn't rain. Instead, we made it to the other side. We all got out as if arriving at life. The cat knew better and stayed in the backseat. The dog ran away. But I went to find you, Samo. I walked and I walked. I looked for B. I looked for something grand, a mausoleum of marble. I looked for something utterly simple and made of wood. I saw the man and my mother talking and opening their hands towards me, and I thought maybe I should give up on you, Samo. Maybe I should dedicate myself to these people. To people and not the love of people. Even though people will betray you. Again and again. At least they're flesh. At least they die. Love and art won't die. Those things haunt. And so, I let the idea of you go. And as I did, there you were. Just like all the others. A regular square of stone. There was a paint brush another lover had placed. And there was your name. I left a stone. Those impossible fruits are what you ghosts like to eat. One of medium size, to represent me. The tour guide told me that's what you ghosts like to eat. So, this is how love lives. Left stones and getting lost and other people's paintbrushes and a mother gently removing her child's spleen. I can keep you safe, better than anybody who ever spent five grand on your crowns and penises. My mother will never give her blessing, but look, we can have a cat together. Futures are only a hill away if you'll take off the condom or the cape, or whatever we humans cover ourselves with when we're afraid.

Love,

End Notes:

p. 12: *Blood Wedding* is a the title of a play written by Federico Garcia Lorca.

p. 13: The title of "Body Logic" comes from: *Hip Logic*, a collection of poems by Terrance Hayes and *The Body's Question*, a collection of poems by Tracy K. Smith.

p. 26: In the prose poem, "To Fall or Fly" the phrase "I want to survive my Diego" comes from the visual artist, poet and actor, Autumn Knight.

p. 50: The title of "Last Yanique Nation" is a retake on Gerald Stern's "Original Stern Country." The last line is from Derek Walcott's "The Schooner *Flight*". The section I take from is this: "I'm just a red nigger who love the sea/(I had a sound colonial education/ (I have Dutch, nigger and English in me/(and either I'm nobody, or I'm a nation."

p. 65: "Traditional Virgin Islands Wedding Verse" was written as an epithalamium for the wedding of Hannah Chadeayne Appel and James Crosby. The form of a Traditional Virgin Islands Wedding Verse requires a direct address to both the bride and groom and the repetition of the word "belong" or its synonym in every verse, save the last two.

p. 67: Samo is a tag name Jean-Michel Basquiat used to refer to himself.

THANK YOU

First and forever, thank you to my children who answer my wishes simply by existing, and to my loving and beloved husband, Moses Djeli McGarrah who continues to be my partner despite the betrayal of my being a poet. Thank you to my readers: Father Britone, Jericho Brown, James Hall, Emily Pérez, Addie Tsai and Anton Nimblett. Thank you to my teachers: Claudia Rankine, Catherine Barnett, David Rivard and dear Deborah Diggs. Thank you the poets: Christian Campbell, Kimiko Hahn, Terrance Hayes, Thomas Sayers Ellis, Major Jackson, Patrick Phillips and Pat Rosal for looking out. Thank you to the poets Eva Lorraine Galiber and Audre Lorde, who wrote poems, so that I could imagine writing poems, too. Finally, thank you to Peepal Tree. Peepal Tree is where I have discovered some of my favourite books of poems. I am joyous that *Wife* is among them.

Thank you to the places where these poems, some in earlier version, have appeared:

H.O.W., Fall 2015: "Dangerous Things"; *Epoch*, Spring 2015: "My brother comes to me", "The Confession of the Five Foolish Brides"; *The Feminist Wire*, Spring 2013: "Dictionary"; *Hot Street,* Spring 2013: "Cock", "Eight Weeks as Frida"; *Poem, Memoir, Story*, Fall 2009: "Zuihitzu" published here as "Zuihitsu for the day I cheat on my husband, to my fiancé"; *Fiddlehead*, Spring 2008: "Gods and Monsters," "Chiron and Astraea"; *Black Renaissance/Renaissance Noire*, Summer/Fall 2007: "To Capture Ghosts", "Body Logic"; *Xavier Review*, Fall 2006: "A poem to mark the day we didn't drive across Texas at night because we were afraid." Published here as "A poem to mark when we were afraid".

ABOUT THE AUTHOR

Tiphanie Yanique is a poet and fiction writer. She is the author of the picture book, *I Am The Virgin Islands*, illustrated by Moses Djeli. Her novel, *Land of Love and Drowning*, won the 2014 Flaherty-Dunnan First Novel Award from the Center for Fiction, the Phillis Wheatley Award for Pan-African Literature, and the American Academy of Arts and Letters Rosenthal Family Foundation Award, and was listed by National Public Radio as one of the Best Book of 2014. *Land of Love and Drowning* was also a finalist for the Orion Award in Environmental Literature. She is also the author of a collection of stories, *How to Escape from a Leper Colony*, which won her a listing as one of the U.S. National Book Foundation's 5Under35. *BookPage* listed Tiphanie as one of the 14 Women to watch out for in 2014. Her writing has won the 2011 Bocas Award for Caribbean Fiction, Boston Review Prize in Fiction, a Rona Jaffe Foundation Writers Award, a Pushcart Prize, a Fulbright Scholarship and an Academy of American Poet's Prize. She has been listed by the *Boston Globe* as one of the sixteen cultural figures to watch out for and her writing has been published in the *New York Times*, *Best African American Fiction*, *The Wall Street Journal* and other places. Tiphanie is from the Virgin Islands and is a professor in the MFA program at the New School in New York City, where she is the 2015 recipient of the Distinguished Teaching Award. She lives in New Rochelle, New York with her husband, teacher and photographer Moses Djeli, and their two children.